May, 80   Sydney

To Frank Krueger

In appreciation of all your help
in selling FPS

From

Peter D. Jones

SYDNEY HARBOUR

Half-title page: From the tip of
Bradleys Head the sunrise dims
the South Head lighthouse beam
in a Sydney summer, and lights a
scene which has enraptured man's
attention long before (and after)
Governor Phillip made this
harbour the site of a British colony.

Endpaper map reproduced by courtesy of
the Under-Secretary for the Department
of Lands, New South Wales

Photographs © LAWRENCE COLLINGS 1978
Text © OLAF RUHEN 1978
First published 1978 by William Collins
Publishers Pty Ltd, Sydney
Type set by Dalley Photocomposition, Sydney
Printed by Toppan Printing Co. Ltd, Hong Kong

ISBN 0 00 216407 8

ON AND AROUND
SYDNEY HARBOUR

LAWRENCE COLLINGS
OLAF RUHEN

Collins SYDNEY·LONDON

Arthur Phillip,
first Governor of
New South Wales.

SYDNEY HARBOUR—
A Paradise of Waters

A MILE OF NAVIGABLE WATER separates the two majestic sandstone jambs of Sydney Harbour's gateway, in summer's light a mile of royal blue from which one looks eastward to the rising sun. The golden light deflects from golden cliffs; more days than not it comes unfiltered through a cloudless sky, still in these latitudes under the benign influence of the Calms of Capricorn. A Mediterranean climate, some say, in a loose description meant to convey the delight of alfresco luxury.

With your back to the dawn you find your field of vision fenced by bush-clad hills separating a complex of bays, their heights sometimes crowned with a sprawl of buildings, mainly for living in. Some settlements line the broader bays and back the beaches, but the main prospect from this entrance is of bush and cliff, and little discloses the sheer size of the city from which the harbour takes its common name.

Perhaps this is the best way to discover this city, this State, this continent: to approach it with the sun behind you on a sparkling morning through these guardian cliffs. I count myself lucky, anyway, to be one of the small and diminishing band for whom this was their first Australian experience, and the occasion has seemed symbolic ever since—the sun's light creating a new day, the welcome fissure in sandstone walls that stretched away to either side as far as the eye conveniently saw, the transition from ocean's intransigence to harbour calm, the ship's progress unveiling piecemeal a testimony to man's domination of the territory he has taken here unopposed: a bustling harbour traffic, an increasing intensity of buildings, roads, wharves, navigational aids, the fabric of settlement—and the almost virgin installations of defence.

Captain Cook, two centuries ago, discovering this coast for the European and Asian record, came this way but resisted the invitation of the entrance. He passed at noon, sailing along in a light southerly after eight days in which he'd had his scientists botanizing in the new land. From a few kilometres at sea as he took his sights (33° 50′ S.) he 'noted a Bay or Harbour wherein appeared to be safe anchorage which I called Port Jackson'. Sir George Jackson was second secretary to the Admiralty and had a sister living at Great Ayton, the village where Cook had been a farm boy.

His brief description induced the Governor of the First Fleet, when Botany Bay proved inadequate for settlement, to investigate the harbour, and here as Stockdale recorded in *A Voyage to New South Wales,* 'Governor Phillip had the satisfaction to find one of the finest harbours in the world, in which a thousand sail of the line might ride in perfect security.

'It runs chiefly in a westerly direction, about thirteen miles into the country, and contains not less than a hundred small coves whose projections afford admirable shelter from all winds. Sydney Cove lies on the south side of the harbour, between five and six miles from the entrance. The necks of land that form the coves are mostly covered with timber, yet so rocky that it is not easy to comprehend how the trees could have found sufficient nourishment to bring them to so considerable a magnitude.'

The maritime organization of the harbour has made shelter no longer the prime contribution of these coves and headlands, but they ensure that, in their favoured neighbourhoods, most of Sydney's people look daily or hourly upon a spectacle of beauty, serene under sunshine and starlight, ruffled into dancing vigour under the east winds of summer afternoons, violently turbulent under the occasional sweeps of the southerlies and offering some balm for the summer heat and winter cold the westerlies bring from the inland.

From the entrance the waterway divides into three arms that to the untutored eyes seem almost equally impressive. First on the right is North Harbour, a complex of perhaps two kilometres in depth. At its centre a low sandy peninsula separates the ocean beaches where Australian surfing began early this century from the harbour beach that was Sydney's first summer resort. At this place Governor Phillip, on his open-boat voyage of search for a settlement site, encountered twenty natives who waded into the water unarmed to accost him, 'received what was offered them, and examined the boat with a curiosity which impressed a higher idea of them than any former account of their manners had suggested'.

Highly pleased with this confidence and manly behaviour Phillip gave the place the name of Manly Cove. It is an older name, therefore, than that of Sydney herself. Besides its sixteen beaches at harbour and ocean side Manly has a windswept clifftop reserve with a wealth of rare native shrubs and native birds, protected to some degree by large quarantine and army establishments from which the public is excluded. With these and an aquarium, a fun fair and beach-bright crowds, Manly has a population that swells to double size every summer, numbering then close to 100,000.

A resort that only a few visitors ever see, and those predominantly the unluckiest, is the quarantine station, almost in the harbour's mouth but sheltered from its frequent turmoil by Cannae Point, just behind the inner North Head, and performing the function of the tonsils for the body of the State, entrapping the advance guards of germ infection. It is impossible to assess the value of this function, whether partly or totally successful, for the preventive work of quarantine is seldom spectacular.

But Australia's quarantine regulations, efficiently applied and especially at this point, did save her from the second and greatest wave of pandemic influenza, a wave that in neighbouring New Zealand was blamed for taking more lives than World War I, just then coming to its end. The ship that conveyed the disease to New Zealand, according to report, was the R.M.S. *Niagara,* and here her name, with hundreds of others, is carved upon the rock, for the detainees here had little else to do.

Often when the physical inactivity drove them to mental creativity, and especially in earlier days, they recorded their experiences in doggerel, and the sandstone offered an undeserved longevity for their efforts. Here in 1838, for instance, a rhymester recorded this still-legible railing against fate.

> *Let weary travellers listen. We tell*
> *The awful treatment that to us befel*
> *On the* Mariposa *many were our woes,*
> *It is a mercy we haven't turned up our toes.*

Since 1831 this has been the official station, a tract of land handy to the harbour entrance and capable of being effectively shielded from contact with the rest of Sydney, but some of the many graves here go back to 1813, and perhaps before that ships were isolated in the beautiful sheltered bay that Phillip named Spring Cove. In spite of the menace of epidemic, and the graves that were a constant reminder of sadness, the station must have been a happy waiting ground for thousands. For here the heathland is rich in wildflowers, many songbirds inhabit the scrub, and the views of harbour and coastline are unexcelled.

Overleaf: The romance of South Sea cruises begins at the Sydney waterside, where Island trade began. Traditionally the city is the metropolis for South Pacific Islanders and the social life of the ocean swings on the Sydney-San Francisco axis. The bright promise of island delight shines from the liner *Oriana* in a harbour dawn.

Directly opposite a similar flora carpets a reserve on the hillside between Dobroyd Head and Grotto Point, still beautiful in spite of a too-frequent modification by bushfire. And between Grotto Point and Middle Head, Middle Harbour stretches away to the north-west and at first sight gives the false impression that it is of lesser extent than the north arm.

Set square behind the harbour entrance is Sydney's most popular harbour beach, Balmoral, a name associated also with adjoining Edwards Beach, where one of hundreds of shark-netted pools gets year-round use. Sometimes in winter, storms from the Tasman Sea thrash through the normally sheltered water with such effect that surfboard riders have taken the crests to the point where the net fences off the pool. An equally violent sea kicks up at Grotto Point.

Behind the beach the followers of Mrs Annie Besant in the Theosophical Society once erected an extraordinarily material testimony to their belief in a new Messiah. It took the form of an amphitheatre in which he would lecture on his appearance, and which could also be used for ballet, drama and religious pageants. It faced the harbour entrance, framed in this vista by the perpendiculars of North Head on the left and the inner slopes of Middle Head, dominated now by an impressive naval hospital, on the right. The responsibility of the Order of the Star in the East, the amphitheatre was completed in 1924 when the Messiah-elect was J. Krishnamurti. In the legend that today persists it was sited to observe the Second Coming, which some prophets declared was about to take place, with an approach through the harbour's magnificent portals. The location could have been significant in a way its builders did not take into account, combining its assembly of nature's sensual delights with a sought-for religious experience.

After Krishnamurti denied in 1929 that he was the vehicle of the new Messiah, and embarked on his own spiritual course, the Order of the Star in the East dissolved, and hopes of enjoying the greatest spectacle of the age were dampened. Interest in the amphitheatre declined and at a later date a prosaic block of red brick flats replaced the temple of faded hopes.

Deeper in Middle Harbour on its northern shores is Clontarf, the sandy beach where on 12 March 1868 a mad Irishman, a self-styled 'bloody Fenian', shot and wounded His Royal Highness, the Duke of Edinburgh, second son of Queen Victoria, in a nearly successful assassination attempt.

Just upstream of this beach a sandspit reduces the width of Middle Harbour and creates the illusion that here it comes to an end. But an opening bridge, in frequent use for the transit of pleasure craft, gives cruising yacht and ferry access to miles more of channels and bays navigable by small craft. Long Bay, Sailors Bay, Sugarloaf Bay, Bantry Bay and the main channel all have a wealth of coves and little beaches. The channels strike deep into the heart of Frenchs Forest, sixteen thousand hectares of flower, bird and animal sanctuary traversed twice daily by the commuters from Sydney's northern beach suburbs.

Only the very fortunate or the very determined have been able to build on these shores, their efforts restricted not only by the proclamation of reserves, but by the steep contours of the harbour banks here and the difficulty of access.

By far the heaviest settlement lines both sides of the main harbour, but particularly its southern shore, centred on Sydney Cove which Governor Phillip pitched on as the site for the first settlement because of the accessible water of the Tank Stream.

From an entrance between South and Middle Heads the main channel turns southward for three or four kilometres before swinging west for the remainder of its twenty-five kilometre length. On Middle Head two tall stone obelisks, one on the shore, one on the hill, give the earliest channel marking for Australia, lining up to mark the best passage through the Heads. Navy and army have divided the whole area of the head and their installations have left the whole coastline very much in a state of nature, though at this point an introduced honeysuckle has replaced much of the native bush and fills the summer air with heady scent.

At Chowder Bay, where American whalers made their favourite dish with a base of the plentiful rock oysters, the army has a base for its small ships arm. The far-famed Sydney rock oysters still grow in profusion but in these great waterways their taste is tainted with the diesel oil of waterborne traffic. Behind the bay is Clifton Gardens, where legend has it that a whaling captain named Clift swallowed the anchor and settled himself ashore to grow the vegetables for his compatriots' chowder. Following this coast for eight or nine kilometres from the obelisk at Middle Head, sometimes scrambling over rocks, sometimes following bush paths, the Sydneysider at leisure remains in the rich relaxation of nature reserves, reaching residential areas again at Little Sirius Cove. Following such routes the harbour's whole coastline stretches in excess of two hundred and fifty kilometres at a rough measure.

Clifton Gardens has been a picnic spot ever since the days when the only access was by water. It still remains a favourite for holiday crowds, with a splendid shark-proof pool for their summer play. By far the main attraction in this area is Taronga Zoo, a thirty-hectare corner of the larger bird and animal sanctuary, Ashton Park. Once reckoned among the world's best zoos, the Taronga Zoo sank into lethargic decline for nearly a quarter of a century after the beginning of World War II. The trouble mainly was a lack of government support. But it has always been bright with flowers, its harbour views are unexcelled, and under the sensitive direction of recent administrators, Ronald Strahan and Peter Crowcroft, it is regaining an honoured place. Its breeding record has been good; it has had great success, for example, with the breeding of giraffes in confined captivity, with its orang-utans and other rare and endangered species, and has an impressive display of Australian avifauna. Included in its tally of a million visitors a year is a large number of school children catered for by its Education Centre. But its once impressive aquarium has fallen on evil days, at least in part because of structural weakness.

In any map of the harbour the zoo area may be seen as the bunched fist behind a long finger pointing south, extending into the tidal current and forming the pivot on which it changes direction to run from south-south-west to west, from east to north-north-east. The tip of the finger is Bradleys Head, named for Lieutenant Bradley who served on *Sirius,* the First Fleet's main escort vessel. In 1841 the authorities seized on its strategic position to begin the installation of a fortress, as the *Sydney Morning Herald* reported on 8 February that year:

'Lest some chance frigate or letter of marque should, in the event of war, think fit to pay us a sort of Paul Jones visit in Sydney, our active and spirited officers have already made preparations for giving them a warm reception such as they may little expect. Our two grand points of defence, Bradley's Head and Pinchgut Island will be within a short time very strongly fortified, under the talented superintendence of Lieutenant-Colonel Barney, and will command the entrance to Sydney. Last week we observed the Government launch actively employed in taking a number of heavy guns to the battery at Bradleys Head, sufficient to blow out of the water the largest ship of the line that may attempt to force a passage. The fortifications at Pinchgut will be ready in a few days to receive a similar supply of heavy guns. This looks, indeed, both warlike and businesslike.'

Pinchgut is one of the most significant of the harbour's fourteen islands and received its common name in the earliest times—a sailor term from windship days of an obstacle that narrowed a channel and made manoeuvring difficult. In another sense the name had a whimsical application when briefly, the island was used as a prison, sharks or the fear of them taking the place of bars. Part of the punishment was the bread and water diet (though the prisoners could augment this with plenty of the world's best oysters) and no doubt they felt the pinch in their bellies at times, or were reputed so to do.

Overleaf: The seamark of Shark Island lies in Rose Bay between Point Piper and Shark Point and clear of shipping lanes. Aborigines bestowed the more appropriate name of Boambilly on this picnic reserve and its poetry may survive.

Today Colonel Barney's picturesque fortifications have mainly a tourist value, though at Bradleys Head a stone pillar marks a precise sea-mile measured from the tower on Pinchgut. Also here as a national memorial is the fighting top of H.M.A.S. *Sydney* which, commanded by Captain John C. T. Glossop R.N., sank the German cruiser *Emden* on 9 November 1914, a major Australian action.

Between Bradleys Head and the point at which the Harbour Bridge spans the waterway and demarcates the outer harbour, several deep coves indent the northern shore. Deepest and most beautiful is Mosman Bay, or Greater Sirius Cove, where the flagship of the First Fleet was careened for strengthening in the earliest days. In 1830, because of the offensive smell of whaleships, the bay, still in its pristine state, was set aside for the equipment of whalers and became the focal point of the local industry. Archibald Mosman (from whom the area takes its name) assumed control and built stone wharves and buildings, one of which, with its entrance flanked by two five-metre rib-bones of a right whale, is still in use. The whale figures prominently in the coat-of-arms of Mosman and its institutions.

Similar ribs form an arch at the harbour entrance to the Royal Sydney Yacht Squadron headquarters at Kirribilli. The three bays which separate these two memorials to a sad industry are Shell Cove, Neutral Bay and Careening Cove. At the first of these, known originally as Hungry Point, oyster shells provided the lime for building mortar. Neutral Bay was set aside from the second year of settlement for the accommodation of foreign vessels. They were anchored at this distance from Sydney partly so they could not easily provide an escape route for the settlement's convicts. Careening Cove, like Great Sirius, was a convenient place for careening vessels for hull cleaning and overhaul.

On Kirribilli Point is Admiralty House, originally the home of Colonel Barney but acquired by the Government in 1885 to house British Admirals and their staffs. Twelve of them lived there in succession until 1913 when the resident Admiral Sir George Patey handed over the house to the Commonwealth Government against the protests of New South Wales. Closed for years as an economy measure the building was made an official residence for Australia's Governors-General in 1947 on the urging of Sir William McKell. Its nearest neighbour, the charming Kirribilli House, was set aside in 1956 to provide a suitable residence for important overseas visitors and has performed this function since, except for a short period when it housed Prime Minister E. G. Whitlam.

Sydney's best known landmarks, the Harbour Bridge and the Opera House, flank her ever-changing waterfront skyline to east and west, and skyline, bridge and theatre all celebrate the triumphs

of human effort. The Harbour Bridge, built in the nine years before 1932 when it opened, permitted the easy expansion of Sydney into the harbour's northern shores, and its design rapidly became an unofficial emblem, a figurative representation of all the brash pragmatic drive that makes up Sydney's character.

But that function has in recent years very largely passed to the Opera House, a unique grouping of four auditoria and supplementary offices and halls under a crown of vaulted spherical segments in gleaming off-white tile, so arranged as to evoke poetical similes—sails, slit magnolia petals, a cockscomb oyster colony—in nearly all references. Its designer, Joern Utzon, won the prize in a competition which attracted 223 entries from architects in 30 countries.

The Opera House stands upon a peninsula of its own formed in past years by the levelling for defence of a hill dubbed the Tarpeian Rock, and the linking of a small island to the mainland there. The quarried cliff behind is capped by the Tudor gothic residence of the State Governor. Its castellations dominate the peninsula that

Popular enthusiasm for colour contributes grandly to the spectacle of sails, especially when yachtsmen spread their spinnakers to following winds.

The suburb of Manly used to advertise its attractions as being 'seven miles from Sydney and a thousand miles from care', and hydrofoils make short work of the distance, supplementing the larger ferries with a frequent timesaving service, and in stormy weather are appreciated for their halving exposure time to wind and wave at the harbour entrance.

divides Sydney Cove, alive with bustling ferries, a passenger terminal and wharves for police launches and island ships, from Farm Cove, a semi-circular centrepiece for the Royal Botanic Gardens beyond, the terminal end of a chain of green parks that give beauty to the city's landward boundaries, and the location of the infant colony's first plantings.

Across Woolloomooloo Bay from Mrs Macquarie's Chair, the headland within the Gardens, another reclamation project linked Garden Island to the mainland at Potts Point, to form Australia's major naval base. This has supplementary installations throughout the harbour: a torpedo factory and wharves for submarines at Neutral Bay, a boom depot in Balls Head Bay, the hospital at Balmoral, the Naval Diving School and Experimental Laboratory at H.M.A.S. *Rushcutter* and a number of other special departments.

The tall buildings of Kings Cross and Double Bay beyond gradually give place to the residential areas of Woollahra, some of them, at Point Piper and Vaucluse and Parsley Bay proclaiming the exclusiveness of luxury. Some of these private houses commemorate events and individuals prominent in Australia's history.

The Rose Bay airport was once perhaps the most exciting of Australia's overseas terminals, where flying boats maintained a busy linkage with the northern hemisphere and some Pacific Islands, but now a flying boat is rare indeed. The reserves continue to take their share of the shores; Shark Island centres the bay and Shark Point, a kilometre north-east, bounds Nielsen Park, another popular picnic spot.

The harbour's sharks have given Sydney a bad reputation and certainly some must always cruise the waters here, yet they have not truly earned the notoriety of hostility to man. Indeed the first settlers to fall victim to a sea animal were killed not by sharks but by one of the whales that are reputedly friendly. Two and a half years after the first landing, on 23 July 1790 Midshipman Ferguson from the *Sirius* and Marines John Bates and Tom Harp and John Wilkins were fishing in a punt when a whale attacked them, as though he knew the devastation the influx of such men would bring to his tribe in southern oceans. He twice lifted the boat from the water and several times crowded it so that they pushed against his body trying for escape, then threw it so high in the air that it smashed. Three men died, Wilkins saved himself with a swim of well over a kilometre. And incidentally this was the first whale seen within the harbour.

Less than twenty people are known to have been the victims of harbour shark attack in two hundred years; on the other side of the scale the shark's reputation has also helped in a great saving of lives from drowning. The harbour swimmer, especially the tyro, keeps close to the shore from this very fear of the shark; the sensuous joys of swimming in these sheltered waters would certainly tempt a great number otherwise to venture beyond depths they can handle.

No one who sees Sydney in the summer months can doubt that water sports provide active participation for more Australians than any other form of recreation. In Sydney the most obvious of these sports, because the most eye-catching, is sailing; on summer days thousands of craft respond to the near-certainty of the afternoon's firm, steady, ten- to fifteen-knot north-easter, generated by the sun-heating of the air above the continent. Sometimes there's the excitement of higher winds, and sometimes the day's sport comes abruptly to a halt on the approach of one of the occasional southerly busters. For these there's always warning but the youngsters fail to heed it.

They sail everything, jinking about on sailing surfboards with eye-catching skill and on and up through the classes, to America's Cup contenders, and cruising yachts. For these latter the Sydney-Hobart ocean race, inaugurated in 1945, has become one of the world classics.

The working-class suburb of Balmain throughout the last half of last century held regattas in which small boats carried incredible areas of sail, especially the eighteen-footers, flat-bottomed open boats crewed by Sydney's toughest breed. The record shows that Plugger Martin, sailing *Zanita,* carried a press of canvas measuring 3,500 square feet, centred on a mainsail 32 feet on the boom. After a 1913 race in which a squall capsized twenty of the twenty-one starters regulations set maximum sail area at 2,800 feet, a figure which has dropped to 1,300 as the eighteen-footer crew has dropped from twelve to fifteen men to a regulation three or four, according to whether you sail in the Flying Squadron or the Sailing League.

Besides sailing, the young Sydneysider sculls, paddles and rows in shells, dinghies, kayaks and canoes and competes in an annual race for bathtubs, most of which have been modified out of recognition. Most of the sculling takes place in sheltered coves west of the Harbour Bridge.

Most of the harbour's ship accommodation is also west of the bridge, major exceptions being passenger and cargo installations at Woolloomooloo and Circular Quay. Inland from this point a major arm of the harbour turns south and is split by the Pyrmont peninsula into Darling Harbour and Johnstons Bay, the latter being resolved by Glebe Island into the Blackwattle, Rozelle and White Bays, all of these, and Walsh Bay at the entrance, well furnished with wharves and piers. Between Walsh Bay and Darling

The barren island of Mattewaye, a favoured fishing perch for Aborigines, became Rock Island and then Pinchgut and, when a picturesque Martello tower replaced the natural rock pinnacle in 1841, Fort Denison. Its guns have never seen action except for the one o'clock cannon fired daily from 1906 to 1942. Captain Clifford Morris sends readings from the automatic tide gauge to Greenwich Observatory in the United Kingdom for world distribution.

Harbour the Port Operations and Communications Centre rises on a slim column eighty-seven metres above sea-level to give the Maritime Services Board's officers a visual command of the harbour traffic.

At Glebe Island and White Bay special wharf facilities cater to the container ships, which have revolutionized general cargo handling to such degree that they spend only a quarter of their time in port, compared to a general average of three-fifths. Just further west at Mort Bay, still hugging the Balmain peninsula, more special wharves have been built to the needs of the roll-on, roll-off ships.

Cockatoo Island stands like a signpost where the channel once again divides into three major arms: Iron Cove, the Parramatta River and the Lane Cove River. A ship-building centre, its significant history began about 1840, when Governor Gipps used it as a keep for convicts withdrawn from Norfolk Island and had them cut bottle-shaped granaries in the sandstone which were so effectively sealed hermetically with well-pitched planking that the weevils, brought incidentally with the grain from India, died in the confinement.

Despite the bustling of Cockatoo, the large areas pre-empted for their needs by industry, commerce, and the service centres like Goat Island where firefloats, tugs and launches have their base, the upper harbour still continues, though not quite so abundantly, the pattern of reserves and holiday places which reflects the Sydneysider's capacity for relaxation. It is a greener Sydney, a more relaxed Sydney than most strangers have been led to expect and, near harbour shores, a city rich with shrubs and trees.

Perhaps the commonest of the native trees is that misnamed the Sydney red gum, an angophora with a bold smooth trunk, pink and dimpled, and frequently with its shape twisted fancifully as its roots and branches adapt to the sandstone habitat. In early summer its peeling bark leaves it with a bright beauty. But the great figs, flourishing in easier terrain and spreading wide from deeply buttressed pedestals, command more admiration.

In these circumstances the birds have resisted fairly well the menace that heavy settlement brings. The shy blue heron, though outnumbered by the gulls and terns, probes the rocks of the less frequented beaches; half-submerged convoys of shags and divers cruise the bays and watch the fishermen on the rocks.

The harbour doesn't provide enough fish to feed its population; the commercial fleets mainly concentrate on prawns and seasonal runs of school fish, but the amateur is always to be found on wharves where notices forbid his activity, on isolated points of rock or on anything that floats, from tenders and rubber dinghies to charter boats well equipped for deep-sea angling.

The happy location for the aesthetically pleasing Sydney Observatory was fixed upon in 1856, displacing an earlier decision to set it on North Shore hill-crests because of the convenience and economy of having it where the dropping of a timeball could give accurate local time and a chronometer check to ships in Sydney Cove, Walsh Bay, Darling Harbour, Gibraltar and Balmain.

The small native animals have shown unexpected powers of survival within the metropolis limits; possums and bandicoots are no rarity, private gardens in most waterfront suburbs house a blue-tongued lizard or two, or even water dragons and rarer reptiles, but a sad fecundity among feral cats has ensured that the bigger varieties of land birds, currawongs, gill birds, crows, kookaburras, magpies and doves, survive better than the dainty blue wrens or other miniature beauties. On the North Shore small flocks of galahs are a common sight as they pick up seeds from the grass in the parks, and little squadrons of joyfully screaming rosellas fly in fast formation.

Like the survivors, the animals of sea and air and land, the Sydneysider has adjusted. He may come from a family seven generations planted on this sandstone; he may have come from the outer ends of the earth, but he accepts without question and without overt gratitude the blessings of his chosen environment, and not the least of them centre on the harbour.

Traditionally a haven is a resting place, a resort where the body can recuperate and the mind deal unhindered with its problems, a place for overhaul and repair; and this haven Sydney was able to offer the questing pioneers. Her fields were not over-fertile, her timber second-grade, the purity of her waters largely dependent on the circumstances that no major rivers ran into them and they opened no effective channel for communication. As an entrepot the harbour was not well placed: it could not compete with the inferior harbour of Melbourne, as, in those early days, its access to its own back country was limited by the sandstone cliffs of the Blue Mountains. But it had beauty, and that of an indestructible kind. With this assurance, men settled here and began to build a nation.

Sydney returns to her past for
Australia Day celebrations at The
Rocks, a suburb which the
residents claim exemplifies the
Australian urban character. A
Cobb and Co. Coach preserved
from early in the century plies for
juvenile delight.

Rowed by a 'convict' crew,
'Governor King' and an escort of
'soldiers' join Australia Day
festivities at a Circular Quay
wharf carrying over its normal
quota of kids and pigeons. Flags fly
at the first landing place.

In 1843 stone from a deep cutting
in Argyle Street, till then
impassable because of a steep cliff
at its centre, was used to form the
seawall at Circular Quay. Because
of thieves and footpads the cutting
had a dark reputation before it was
bridged for the highway overhead.
Lower down the street the Bond
Stores perform a new function as a
trendy craftwork centre.

Overleaf: Peak-hour traffic
converges as the expressway tapers
to the Harbour Bridge crossing.

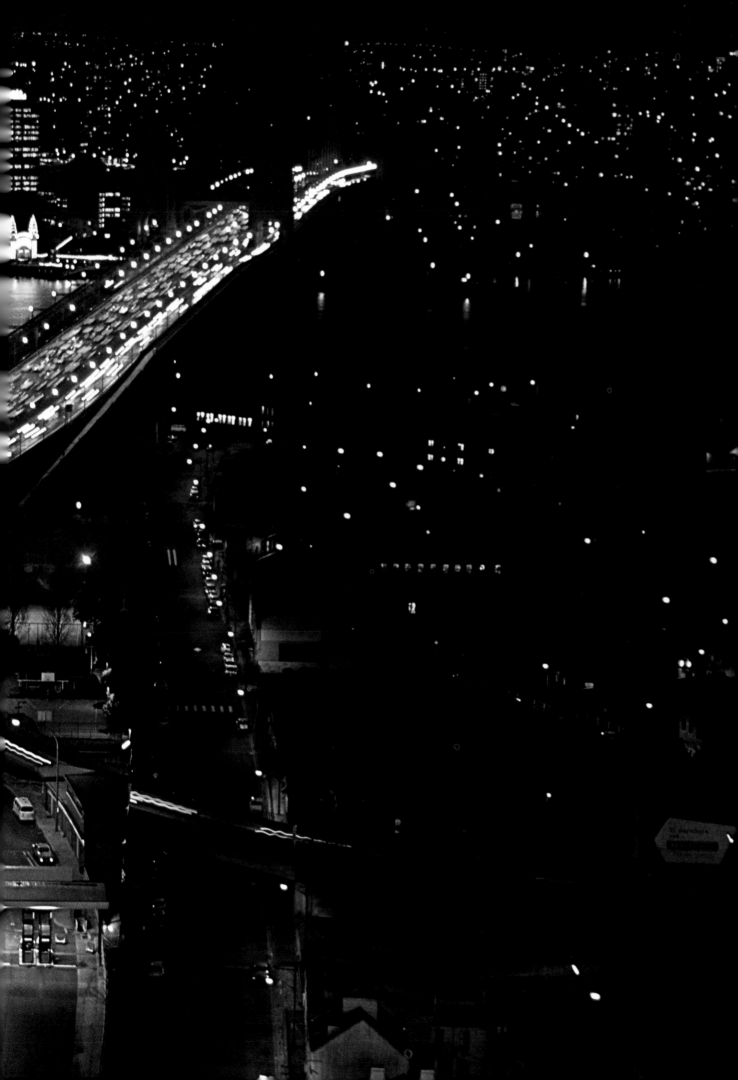

All around the Quay: Kite-flying on the Fourth of July, children sitting on the sun-warmed iron of Dawes Point guns, expectant Sydneysiders waiting for the *Arcadia* to berth and their relations to come ashore.

The Opera House designer's iconoclastic approach to traditional forms has provided an aesthetic treasure-house of new and pleasing patterns.

Happiness is a scattering of gulls. The silver gull is the most common of shore birds all round Australia and her neighbours, and perhaps the most beautiful.

Overleaf: Banksia ericifolia was one of the first specimens collected by Joseph Banks after Cook's discovery of Australia's east coast. From the top of the AMP Centre, the State Government House occupies the foreground of a harbour view.

41

The baths at Woolloomooloo Bay in the heart of Sydney were named for Andrew ('Boy') Charlton, a popular blond lifesaver who three times here beat the great Swede Arne Borg, a swimmer who established the record for breaking the most world records (thirty-one). Visitors to the Art Gallery of New South Wales look across the baths to a view of the Naval Base and a cruising tourist launch explores all the harbour's offerings.

Workers make an early morning start at the Garden Island Naval Base, where one of the less warlike exhibits is the figurehead portraying Queen Victoria, salvaged from the clipper ship *Windsor Castle*.

VICTORIA

Looking almost due north from
Point Piper the quiet vista of the
harbour's upper reaches is
underlined by a launch's wake.
Looking west, the sun sets over the
approaches to the Harbour Bridge.

Marinas in dozens of sheltered spots serve the waterborne holidaymakers of the city, as does this one, the Royal Motor Yacht Club's marina at Rose Bay. *Top left:* An experiment-minded sportsman aquaplanes on a circular disc in the bay. *Lower:* Built in 1902 the venerable steam yacht *Lady Hopetoun* served the Commissioners of the Harbour Trust as an inspection vessel, was taken over by the Maritime Services Board and, as one of the oldest steamers active in the world is, with her stylish lines, a pleasing feature of the water scene.

Overleaf: The start of the deep-water classic, the Sydney-Hobart yacht race, has become the major sporting event on Boxing Day, and spectators who are unable to get waterborne to farewell the contenders line every lookout on the cliffs and headlands.

Using the snorkel for sub-surface breathing in the shallows has added another dimension of delight for the devotees of harbour pleasures. At Shark Bay a sandy beach breaks the harbourside line of rocks and a large shark-proof enclosure protects the bathers. From this vantage the summer sun goes down behind the city skyline.

The eye-catching spinnakers of
three yachts racing neck and neck
near Shark Bay beach. Around the
point, sandstone rocks once
presented an attractive image to
thirsty seafarers, who named it
'Bottle and Glass', but nearly two
centuries of storms have altered the
outline.

Only the total fire bans that
drought conditions sometimes
impose on the Australian in
summer, when the westerlies blot
up all moisture and the shrubs are
like tinder, stand between the
Sydneysider and his barbeque.
They are among the few bans he
normally respects. Most beach
councils ban dogs from the sands;
most dog-owners ignore them.

Overleaf: Rising to the occasion of
its best spectacles the harbour
forms a superlative staging for a
Royal visit. Excited escorts convoy
the Royal Yacht *Britannia* and the
Queen's launch.

Very early morning used to be the busiest part of the day for Watsons Bay when for many years it was the point at which pratique was given incoming vessels. At this time it was inhabited mainly by pilots, signalmen, port officials and fishermen. Today its main offering is relaxation and it is a haunt of the amateur fisherman. Skin divers with scuba gear move out to favoured grounds.

The harbour's offerings of varied
pleasures range from the
windsurfer's fine control of mast,
sail and body in instant response to
the static joy of the sunbaker. A
short distance from the nudes on
Lady Jane Beach members of the
Sydney Game Fishing Club weigh
in a shark on the Watsons Bay
wharf.

Overleaf: Everything that can float
accompanies the departure of
racing yachts for Hobart and
(pages following) the fans look
down from North Head upon a
crowded square mile of sail.

RMS LUSITANIA
JULY 21st 1895
PERCY E. RAYMOND CHIEF OFFICER
NIEL CAMPBELL CHIEF ENGINEER
GEORGE A. HARRIS 2
ROBERT RENTOUL 3
L.M. FALKNER 4
W.H. CLARKE 5
W.T. HOGG 6 COOK
J. STEWART BOILERMAKER SCULPTOR

O.S.N.C.
ARMISTICE
H.M.A.T.S
RIO PARDO
JULY - AUG
1919

R.M.S. NIAGARA
INFLUENZA
OCT. 1918

APRIL 24th 1897
R.M.S. HIMALAYA.
E.H. GORDON   COMMANDER
F.W. BURGESS   PURSER
L. INSOLL   Asst PURSER
E. BUSH   CH. STEWARD
B. CROWTHER   BARMAN
J. DESBOROUGH   Str KEEPER
C. SOPER   Hd WAITER
S. SMITH   2d WAITER
F.T. HALL, F. OSBORNE, T. RIVERS
H. CANARD, C. CANARD, E. MOSS
J. CARRICK, W. UNDERHILL
W. COUGHLAN, SCULPTOR.

Over the years detainees at the quarantine station have filled their time recording their ordeals upon the rocks. But from the heights where some of their companions lie buried they could watch the busy traffic of the harbour entrance, or study an amazingly varied flora, here represented by *Actinotus helianthi*, the flannel flower, a vigorous perennial which grows to one metre and can be cultivated.

Overleaf: Across the harbour is the suburb of Manly.

Left: People enjoying the sights of Manly.

Rainbow lorikeets, the most brilliant and perhaps the noisiest of Australian parrots, seem happy to share their haunts with people.

Grotto Point divides North from Middle Harbour.

Overleaf: A lorcha—European-type hull, Chinese top-hamper—sails towards Middle Harbour; a flotilla of skiffs awaits a race start off Clontarf Beach where Queen Victoria's second son was shot and wounded, and the Spit Bridge opens for the passage of a ferry-load of sightseers.

The deep colour of harbour waters
proclaims the summer season, but
an increasing problem is that of
boat accommodation. Marinas,
such as the one behind the Spit,
cannot be enlarged or multiplied
indefinitely, and launching ramps
for vehicle-towed small craft
require large parking areas on
valuable harbourside land.

The upper reaches of Middle
Harbour plunge deep into nature
reserves where angophoras, the
so-called Sydney red gums, are
amongst the most striking of the
trees that flourish in the poor soil
of this Hawkesbury sandstone
country. Botanical interest in the
dagger bush (*Hakea teretifolia*)
centres in the unusually shaped
woody fruits.

Folly Point acquired its name
when an Irishman used sea water
to mix the mortar for his stone
house because it was readily
available. When the house fell
down he repeated the mistake. The
view he didn't enjoy took in
Quakers Hat and Figtree Point. In
the next bay sea scouts have a
headquarters in bush which in
springtime is redolent with the
perfume of *Acacia suaveolens,* the
sweet-scented wattle.

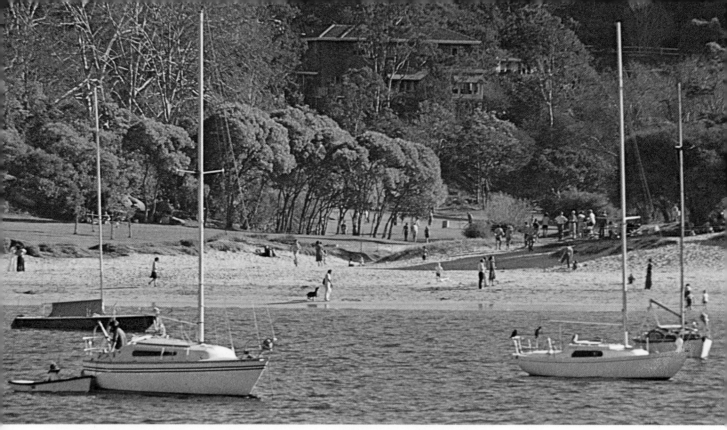

For more than half its boundaries, the suburb of Mosman has some of the most picturesque shores in the harbour. Chinamans Beach, named for the long, slender oysters (like extended fingernails) that are called Chinaman's nails, is a haunt of artists and children. Another artist has set up her easel at Ashton Park, where the reserve includes Taronga Zoo and curiosities like this sandstone emplacement which once held a cannon that commanded harbour channels. Huge trees shade a barbecue at Balmoral.

Overleaf: Grey days have their own beauty.

Nearly all of Bradleys Head is given over to reserves with shore-following paths threading cool groves. The native fuchsia, *Epacris longiflora*, is one of the commoner floral joys.

Overleaf: The Clipper Race, England to England via Sydney, here starting on its second leg, attempts to beat the times the clippers set more than a century ago.

Taronga Zoo is making determined efforts to regain the reputation it once had of being among the world's finest. Among its successes is the breeding of giraffes in close captivity. Australia has become the main source of supply for the Arabian camel.

Overleaf: Fortunate in its site the zoo affords patrons unsurpassed views across the harbour channels.

These shores of Little Sirius Cove are on the same reserve as Taronga Zoo.
Left: Musgrave Street Wharf (Mosman Bay) is on the Mosman ferry route.

In 1863, the year after nineteen yachtsmen formed the Sydney Yacht Club, the Prince of Wales accepted the office of Patron and the Squadron prefaced its title with the word 'Royal'. Forty years later it leased 'Carabella' on Wudyong Point. A feature of the harbour, its three acres on Careening Cove (top right) have given space, though probably never enough, for its installations. *Right:* Wharf-side fishing is a familiar sight to Sydneysiders.

Forming the apex of a broad-based
isosceles triangle of which the base
points are the Opera House and
Fort Denison, Admiralty House
accomplishes its practical function
with a show of beauty which
includes its first-floor verandahs
supported on arched colonnades,
lawns and gardens that seem ever
at their best and a covered
walkway leading down to its own
launch dock.

Overleaf: Foreign vessels were once segregated in Neutral Bay for in the days before telegraph and radio no one knew whether the national relationship was one of war or peace. Submarine wharves beside the torpedo factory suggest preparedness, but the spirit of holiday invests the Olympic swimming pool, the crowded ferry and the Gallipoli Legion Bowling Club under the Harbour Bridge at Milsons Point.

Lavender Bay waters reflect the dancing lights of Sydney's Luna Park playground.

Under threat of storm or placid in still air, in any of its moods the harbour's spell is difficult to resist.

Alexander Berry, a Scot from
Fifeshire who became one of
Australia's first millionaires,
married the sister of his partner
Edward Wollstonecraft whose
210-hectare grant on the North
Shore included Berrys Bay and
(overleaf) Wollstonecraft or
Kerosene Bay. In the reserve on
Balls Head which separates them
boronia grows at the foot of the
scribbly gums. The bays named
after the partners once centred the
boatbuilding trade and some of
this activity persists.

Goat Island, a five-hectare rock dome a kilometre west of the Harbour Bridge had its first stone buildings erected by convicts between 1833 and 1838, including the (lower right) very solidly built powder house, now used as a storehouse. Sir Richard Bourke was then Governor. The island is now the principal depot for firefloats, tugs, barges and other harbour-service craft.

Overleaf: Darling Harbour at sunset.

Sailing ships are rarer visitors now, but sea scouts had an opportunity to get the feeling of earlier days when it was mooted to turn the barquentine *New Endeavour* into a sail-training vessel. *Right:* The brigantine *Eye of the Wind* berthed at Circular Quay to pick up a crew for a world cruise.

In the past, beauty has been too often sacrificed to utility, but the Illoura Reserve on the Balmain waterfront celebrates a reversal of the trend. In 1970 when the

Maritime Services Board closed this one-hectare depot for storage of piling and heavy timbers, the commissioners made a gift of it to the public and enhanced it with

constructions for children's play, utilizing surplus and sub-standard timbers. Nearby the Glebe Island Rowing Club holds a regatta in Blackwattle Bay.

Industry demands its share of harbour frontages as in the coal-loading and storage facilities on Balls Head Bay, a corner of Wollstonecraft on the North Shore. Most is concentrated in the southern arms which also shelter all the commercial fishermen. Container wharves front Johnstons Bay. All transport activities come under the direct control of the Port Operations and Communications Centre on Millers Point.

Overleaf: Circular Quay centres the waterborne movements of people.

Festivities on Australia Day commemorate the proclamation by Governor Phillip of the new colony on 26 January 1788. The celebrations centre on Circular Quay and The Rocks adjoining, and include a fishing competition.

Overleaf: The festivities end with a fireworks display, the pyrotechnic brillance of which lights the sky and is reflected in the sea.